ice cream melts

nnamdi godson osuagwu

Front cover photograph by Chidiadi Ugorji

Interview by D.Shanks

Interview Location: Church of St. Marks, Brooklyn New York

Printing and design by

Falcon Books
San Ramon, California

ISBN: 978-0-9797480-0-4

Published by
Ice Cream Melts Publishing
info@IceCreamMelts.com

PRINTED IN THE UNITED STATES OF AMERICA

Acknowledgments

This project would not have been completed without the constant source of inspiration that I received from the people around me. Thanks to all those that I currently love and once loved.

Contents

The Beginning

Why does ice cream melt?

Scientifically speaking, the melt-down process can be understood through analyzing the structure of ice cream. Ice cream is made up of air, fat, foam, ice crystals and emulsifiers. An emulsifier is an agent that can be added to substances that do not normally mix e.g., water and oil. Emulsifiers, such as polysorbate 80 are added to give ice-cream its smooth consistency by preventing clumping, when fats (usually milk) are added to the mixture. The air is formed in ice-cream through the whipping action needed to create it. The ice crystals are formed through the deep freezing process. During the meltdown phase the ice crystals are the first to liquefy. At this point the ice cream has not officially melted. The next phase is the collapse of the fat-stabilized foam structures. The collapse rate is directly controlled by the added emulsifiers. The less emulsifiers, the quicker the collapse rate and on the contrary; the more emulsifiers the slower the collapse rate.

Basically speaking, ice cream melts because life is complicated. Things can be going great, you just got married, you just got a promotion, you just got a new car, you are healthy, and then all of sudden something goes drastically wrong. The marriage ends in divorce. The promotion turns into a lay off. Someone crashes into the new car while it is parked. The doctor discovers that you have a terminal disease. At any point, sometimes for unexplainable reasons, life's high moments can turn into very low moments. That transition from life's highs to lows is the melting process of ice cream.

Words Writing Words

A connection of words
formed from a strike
onto paper, miraculous
in nature, unlike no other
still thrills me, how the words dance
communicate in their own special way
a life of their own
free to express thought
provoke action and inspire
the uninspired, left to dwindle
down a spiral path of nothingness
resurrected from the depth
of obscurity, coming to understand
the perils of the world through another
from being, one or many
set out to change
scary to deviate from the norm
brave soldiers not of fortune
but of the truth or their version
perspectives from all
funneled through words
to produce masterpieces
that will inspire more to come

Excerpts from Conversations with the Author:

> *"I think some people put themselves in these boxes, and then they get claustrophobic and they can't get out, it's like the weirdest paradox"*

The Mother

Envy

You are a reminder
of everything that
I could have been
or should have been
as cute as you
can be just can't
remove the fact
that your existence
is premature in my life
sort of stunted
my high-powered goals
now my dreams
don't match my age
no longer identical
used to laugh
at my friends
always saying
that can't be me
that'll never be me
then I met him
yes him
a pollinator of flowers
pretty wild flowers
he helped blossom
captivating mentally
a physical wonder
I see you in him
maybe that's why
I hate you
and love you
all at once
just wanted more
out of both our lives
envious of you
you still have a chance

A Good Man

Mama has a new friend
sweetheart
after your poppa left us
don't you think
it was time to move on
this one is a good man
he likes you so much
treats you like his own
little princess
I see the way he watches you
that is love in his eyes
why are you so scary
leave you alone for a second
then comes the tears
you can trust him
mama will be right back
don't be sad
he told me that you were good
today and everyday
happy he doesn't mind
babysitting for me
he actually seems to enjoy it
you should be happy
you have yourself
a new father figure
a man in the house
it has been a long time
baby don't go ruining this for me
I really need him
mama finally found herself
a good man

Fiberglass Crib

I rubbed my stomach
with pride and laughter
happy and ready
to give birth
to the future
sitting and thinking
about the what ifs
hopeful dreams from a woman
that started out far
from her current situation
just found out
it will be a boy
maybe a king
a surgeon, lawyer, general
political lead us and we will follow
we need more that's for sure
in a world where
opportunity is a commodity
yet he chose something different
caught up in helping the family
when he was helping himself
to the spoils of war
street captive of politics
not being freed anytime soon
so we talk between glass barriers
over a phone
can't even touch my baby
reminds me of when he was born
watching him through a fiberglass crib
twenty two years later
we are at the same place

Just Getting Up

Getting up these steps
boy, are you heavy
especially with the stroller
ok just pick it up
hug sweetie's little carrying case
bend the knees
all in one try
just lift
there we go
walking up each step
carefully, yet swiftly
finally there
slide the card
through the turnstile
pull the bar around
without going through
Miss, excuse me
the gate
please open the gate
tap the window for me please
yes, over here, goodness
finally in
now another set of steps
same process
hug, bend, lift, step
walk up and stop
no train still
hear it coming
now I see it
excuse me
no need to push

a seat right by the door
turn the carriage around
about to sit
No, he didn't
just take the seat
like it was his born right
he couldn't even imagine
what I did to get here
calm down
save your energy
the day has just begun

A Good Marriage

Woke up
and felt nothing
looking at him
sleeping peacefully
after all of the lies
cheating, other women
while I'm here
aged passed my years
gave birth to his offspring
does he even know
that I thought of ending
what he values most
or even ruining what
he takes for granted
but I still love this fool
and he just seems to stay
wonder why he didn't leave
yet we take a good picture
that our families like
to hang up
on the walls
of old houses
making them look new
using us as the models
to a perfect union
of two adults
one of which
has no self control
seems hard only for him
but my infidelities had nothing
to do with a wanting
to be touched
or wanting to touch someone other than him
just basic attention
in the form of compliments
and appreciation of my
top to absolute bottom
and that is how
I define satisfaction

Heels

These heels hurt
but girl they look
so good on me
walking, standing up
and watching others
calves showing
dress flowing
a little past the knees
watching, aren't you?
I see it
in your eyes

that was me
as a young women
older now
wearing flats
not impressed anymore
orthopedic surgery
limited my options

Long Day, Pretty Tired

Wake up honey
time to get the kids ready
baby, it's your turn
you slept in yesterday
ok, I'll do it
as usual

Let your sister bathe first
Come eat breakfast
Sweetie, start getting your clothes
Ready for breakfast, your plate is ...
Mommy will be right back
Need to get ready for work
Ok everyone in the car
Your Dad just left
Yes, he has another early meeting
Your Dad will pick you up after practice

You can't? I need to get dinner
Ok, I'll pick them up

ok guys, into the car
need to get home
and get dinner ready
start getting ready for bed
so I guess I'm washing the dishes
love you both too, goodnight
so tired, need sleep
Honey, how was your day?
how was my day, are you serious?
taking a shower and going to bed

what a day, need sleep
baby, please stop
tonight is not good
I'm really tired
don't have the energy
maybe I would
if you would just
help a little more

The Pacifier

Wake up in the morning
and you are there sleeping
leave for work
and you are there sleeping
call from work
and you are there sleeping
call after lunch
and you are there, but not alone
come back from work
and you are watching TV
cook dinner
and you eat in front of the TV
ask if you got any leads
and you say that you made some calls
ask about an interview
and you say no one called yet
about to go to sleep
and you are on top of me
Yes, it feels good
but I am officially turned off
this is not how my father
treated my mother
you have all the makings
of a small boy
that is being taken care of
by his guardian
if that is the case
this relationship is molestation
you are not standing
but being carried around
and I am pacifying you
wiping your ass
and even burping you

can't even walk yet
just crawling around the house
crying when you don't get your way
not grown still teething
when I wake up
hours after you had your pleasure
you will be there no longer
your bags will be outside
and the locks will be changed
I think it is time
to give you up for adoption

Mrs. Unidentified

The street corner cried
as she slept on it
bare skin touching
the raw cold concrete
soaking up all the negativity
grime and soulless memories
the corner is a taker
of energy, arguments loose change
donations of blood sweat and tears
now someone has discovered
how to take from the collector
a sad exchange of events
as the corner released
she engulfed lumps
at times seemed frozen
then she motioned
with her hands out
no one to touch
only a cup to hold
some that past gave looks
others gave a little
of what they had last night
and earlier in the day
she now heard and felt
all that is normal
in this intersection
of angles and deceit
concurrently taking in toxins
shedding her clothing
and her hair became unkempt
motionless and finally noticed
by a kind stranger
offering life in a bag
big enough to fit her presence
Mrs. Unidentified was someone's mother

Mommy's Flowers

A seed was planted
and a flower grew from
within the depths
of a youthful soul
as the flower grew
I watered it
and gave it sunshine
soon that flower
blossomed into a full bush
with long stems
amazing to watch
proud that it came from me
added more meaning to my life
filled my soul with love
then one sunny day
as peace rained over
the lands we occupied
one angry passerby
came along
and forcibly stepped
on my pretty flowers
grinding them into the ground
he then just walked away
leaving my flowers dying on the ground

Excerpts from Conversations with the Author:

> *"I think aging is a beautiful thing, right? But I think one of the saddest things is regret when you're older, because you have a limited amount of time to correct it."*

The Father

Sum Of Life

Is it possible
to trace each step
recounting the most
granular of experiences
which sums up the life
that is known
sort of like
retracting expunged food
through the digestive system
spitting out a perfectly
made dinner
which is then passed
through the chef's skillet
 back into the store
loaded on the trucks
shipped to the farm
and back into the earth
grown to younger
young enough not to exist
by doing so
time has been traveled
even if it is only for a second
only captured through pictures
or a photographic memory
the sum of life through thought
flashes of life before death
flashes of life through a father
staring at his first born
through the womb of his lover

Regrets of an Old man

Just sit here
in long dazes
engulfed in my own loneliness
a space where thoughts are idle
thinking of everything
and nothing at once
no one comes around
to see this old man
just here losing focus
on that point beyond
with another blink
eyes water and another sip
of the brown juice is tasted
the wetness dampen my lips
it was hard not being around
for those that needed me
the most in my youth
something always came up
I was doing it for them
really for myself
ok, for all parties involved
no one sees that struggle
just missed birthdays and graduations
an old man's regret can be
the cruelest thing to bear
due to the time limitations
of correcting past mistakes
with time, wounds only got deeper
hard for me to close them now
permanent scars on adults
who taught their offspring

not to play with sharp objects
trying to tell them
I am dull now
have no more pain to give
not as mobile as I once was
just sit here most days
drink when the nurse is away
this is my new sanity
hands shake with nervousness
when picking things up
so I keep it grounded
just sitting here

Daddy's Girl

Daddy's little girl
I try to find traces
of your mother
during every interaction
listening and carefully
examining your gestures
maybe that's why
I'm so hard on you
you see, I don't like her
and never wanted
anything to do with her
it was an experience
in isolation
when the world froze
and a debt was paid
a reaction for things
done long ago
a past prior to
your existence in the world
now you are here
through a person that
I neither know nor care for
what should be done?
how do we proceed?
you were not made
out of love
but something else
can I love you fully
without thinking of the person
from which you came
and still influences you

in multiple ways
a father's only hope
is his children
for them he sacrifices all
but can you be
a link between
two worlds at war?

Ran into a Memory

Undoubtedly stressful
to come home
and watch loved ones
struggle just to eat
bills are greeting cards
sent monthly from friendly
agencies reminding you
of that long-term commitment
work is not fun
and menial in nature
yet it is done
more so for your dependants
than for yourself
pressure boils
like hot water within a screwed pot
one day as the hot liquid
leaks from the side
echoes of loud noises
are heard from the bedroom
where a staged argument
started to provoke an action
which led to children crying
and asking a lonely women
where has their father gone
she looks at them
eyes teary
and simply states
he'll be back soon
but soon never came
until the children were adults
looking at an older man
bearing a resemblance
and they no remembrance

Another Man

As I lay beside
and watch something so
beautiful right next to me
thinking of my family
and how much I love them
remembering first walks
and laughs around the dinner
tables loaded with food
and the lovely smiling faces
thinking they would never
understand this feeling
that I am experiencing
at this moment
deeper than their comprehension
most people turn away
and couldn't even
imagine these feelings
for another so completely
engulfing my existence
I am a man
is that so hard to believe?
all man, my wife can tell
you stories and stories
so does that take away
from me lying
next to another man?

Father Don't

The paycheck has ceased
to exist in this household
As I look at my pregnant wife
feeding the youngest of three
children that need so much
no longer the provider
now just another to feed
all I wanted was to be in control
and the center of their world
the stress, they don't understand
Can't seem to figure out
how to proceed
need to call it quits
and abandon this life
thinking what will they do without me
how would they go on
and survive in this cold
frigid world without
their protector and champion
not fair to leave them
alone without the center
piecing together a way
out of this existence
need to plan carefully
woke up early
still dark out
took the axe
once used for chores
and started from oldest
to youngest
my beautiful wife

she was first
it took me four strokes
walking to each room
and ending what I aided in creating
so beautiful
they were so at peace
this is for them
it will be better
only in the long run
only a few will understand
that is now done
only one more
as I took a loaded pistol and squeezed

Happy F Day

Just another day
for me to go through
but they put so much
emphasis on this yearly event
guess it feels good
when you have something stable
with a firm foundation
but what about those that don't
spend the day accepting
phone calls from everyone
but the one that matters
asking the same questions
what are you doing today
your response
have a couple of errands
to run or run into
one even poses the question
did she call you
as your heart drops
you say the obvious
I was not expecting a call
now at a bar to drown
those pitiful feelings
down a shot of something
strong is what you need to be
in order to maintain
rather numb the feelings
it now feels comfortable
to escape into another world
away from the everyday
that the sun will wake up

then they call
in the early morning
talking about
monetary monthly obligations
and you thought
they were calling to say
happy father's day

Nagging

It's an indiscriminate sound
that turns into a series of words
echoed in and around
the most inopportune times
mainly present in people
who exchange some,
if any, kind of fluid-like gestures
sometimes ignoring can assist
but doesn't save
or solve real issues
in the present
a quick remedy
just breathe relief
seconds have passed
and still the remarks
about what happened
could be a day
could span weeks
some distant time
which leads into other
topics of discussion
as chalk screeching
against a dry board
understatement of the year
the annoying sound of nagging

Shutting Down

At what point
did that happen?
was it at birth
or maybe during preschool?
was it in high school
or maybe even college?
at the first job
or at my wedding?
during the birth
of my beautiful baby?
at some point
a man learns
to suppress feelings
show little
to no emotion
that's when the smile fades
the face becomes smooth
wrinkle-free
a lot of words
transform into one
or maybe two if lucky
it's called shutting
down for a life moment
something to deal with
makes some cry
and let out emotion
but this man does not
seems out of place
while others lament freely
he deemed himself
the foundation of the house
unshaken and unmoved
he just stands there
half dazed wondering
when did he become
so cold and solid

Reversed

When did it become different?
she started working late
she started buying more lingerie
we don't have as much physical
interactions of pleasure
she is always tired
random wrong numbers
and dropped calls
conversations are not as in depth
real basic with an unbreakable surface
started to look at me differently
when I misplaced my income source
stay at home now
watch the kids and cook
her plate is on the table
but she is late once again
only to arrive with a full stomach
any questions about her whereabouts
are greeted with accusations
of jealousy and then flipped
to make me feel guilty
she preaches how she takes care
of the family and provides
I tell her that
I do my part also
she just shakes her head
and walks away from the discussion
so we keep silent
and don't bring up the obvious
one day before leaving for work
she asks that I ponder

the age-old question
what if it were reversed
as I lie here
staring at the white-coated ceiling
of a luxury hotel
with my secretary
draped over my chest
ignoring the constant calls
resonating music from a cellular device
with the words HOME on the caller id

Play Nice

They all keep asking
for life, material objects,
health of loved ones
dreams fulfilled, more and more
a never ending list of requests
not knowing or forgetting
that all have me within
to seek and become
yet few exercise that option
this place was for you,
my children, to be fruitful
and multiply in happiness
but it was not enough
siblings finding differences
among each other and
noticing the smallest of variations
coming together to enslave
and murder your own kin
such things
can break a father's heart
as he tries to provide
giving all that he can
life which is the greatest gift
taken for granted
brothers and sisters
competing to be the favorite
in the eye of their father
but he loves all the same
hard to believe
so some are punished and ridiculed
just for believing that there

is a different path to their father's heart
it is big enough for everyone
but some would rather have it all
so for now
I stand back
and watch my children play
among each other
just hoping that
they play nice

Excerpts from Conversations with the Author:

> *"The goal was to speak from their perspective because these people don't really have a voice."*

The Daughter

Magic Man

The magic man
made her childhood disappear
only thirteen
and already an object
desired by grown men
so the magic man
snapped his fingers
and she fulfilled
lustful fantasies
strangers became friendly
long enough to break
an aerobic sweat
lying there
thinking of a youth sold
not even to the highest bidder
among the crowd
mouths salivating
as she stares at them
trying hard
not to look directly
no need
for additional provocation
help not even a phone call away
all who could, didn't
the magic man
took care of them
he owns her and others
tears from a flower
watered the earth
from which it was grown
now a tree
with leaves falling
bark chipping
roots of sadness
stemmed her growth

Boy Toys

A few see your emotional state
as fragile delicate
to be handle with care
unfortunately others
kick you around
off balance
you fell from the truck
and were picked up
only to be thrown
on a door step
left standing
and waiting
until he arrives
then you were taken inside
opened up quickly
he ripped off the packaging
smiled at the gift
happy at first
used you a few times
almost broke you
got tired of playing
then flung you
into the closet
now you're in a corner
stacked up against
other used toys

Female Friend

They consider me a friend
one of the boys
but I am not a boy
just a girl with a lot
of male friends
they confide in me
and laugh with me
I am their peoples
talking about other chicks
that they dealt with
or are currently dealing with
or maybe just find attractive
asking for advice
from a feminine point
viewing nothing
not even thinking
for a second
that I might look
want to touch
be touched by them
in a more than a friendly way
kind of sad
I know the truth
they are not attracted
to me in that way
heard that before
too much pride
to even bring up
so I'll settle
for this special role
that the other girls
don't seem have
I bet they envy me
I sure do envy them

Little Girls

Little girls
on their way to school
admiring an old friend
as she came to visit
during a long lunch
everyone gathered around
hands touching
eyes gazing
at her new life
that she brought
from the depths
of her small cavity
all saying
I want one too
he is so cute
shy by all of the attention
the newborn cried
for his guardian
as she picked him up
her friends smiled
happy and envious
of their old friend
they returned to class
after the long lunch break
their old friend strolled
her pride and joy
back home and watched TV
for the remainder of the day

Not Satisfied

We have twenty three hours
and thirty minutes
left to be humans
but we can't talk
or even bear looking
at what was so beautiful
a little bit ago
feelings of emotion
questions of satisfaction
so charming before
convinced me of a realness
that seemed forgotten
a gentleman
that's far from gentle
I'm a woman
with so much more
but you were driven
to only see one side
thought you were bigger
· or it meant more
was it only to me
one-sided mental conversations
left wondering
maybe it was too soon
or if something was done
Did I speak out of turn?
a forever question mark
I guess this is it
and no
I'm not satisfied

Ok You Do That

I listen to him
he thinks he's so cool
half drunk at the bar
talking to me
ok, you do that
ok, great
you make that much
wonderful, good for you
that's what you drive
and you live there
nice neighborhood
over yonder
such a good catch
yet you are here
alone and drunk
at the bar with me
after you talked
to her over there
what a way
to start a relationship

Real In the Field

It's real in the field
of lost dreams
and high-water pants
no beds
blankets on the floor
shivering from the cool
night breezes into the bones
skin practically painted on
camp fires of laughter
that heat is used for heat
joyous occasions
are a rarity
smiles of mediocre sorrow
as you walk past
the living tombs of disgust
walking zombies of the night
avoiding shadows in daylight
a slight glimpse of humanity
chuckles as you look in the mirror
fixing your lipstick
against your plump lips
not naturally constructed
but otherwise perfect
sharp as the crease
in your designer trousers
that hang down
as the wind blows
flapping propellers which carry you
to another place where problems
are so confusing to rationalize
when other parts of the field
are so real

RIP Kat

A special friend
intimate in nature
called one day
and talked to me
about life and all it stood for
and all it fell for
she apologized for all negativity
said she felt responsible
nonchalantly I accepted
the apology that rose from
the crevices of her inner being
goodbyes were said
the conversation ended
a week later the news hit
she was no longer with us
her energy was sucked
away by her own hand

Skinny World

I feel fat
in a skinny world's body
unnoticed by most
that only notice
the majority's beauty
low self esteemed
by those that notice
my many insecurities
from family to friends
not only what they say
but how they treat
others that are far
from my physical appearance
it's everything
and I am everyone
at least to those
that are imperfect
in a perfect world
where perfection comes
on magazine covers
TV shows and movies
people like me
don't stand out
or stand out just
enough not to be mentioned
the opening credits
are rolling
and I'm handing out
popcorn dreams
forgive me
forgetting I'm human
in the way
and obstructing your view
of the main event

Staring at These Two

I stare at these two
amazed and curious
both at once
wondering how it works
if it works
and when it works
both of the same cloth
yet different in nature
observing others
observe them
fascinating are we
of life and ourselves
all taking from each other
pieces that remind us
of our inner beings
trading souls daily
rarely free enough
to be ourselves
in all of the splendor
of living life
then I stare at these two
and now I understand

Young Girl Grown Men

She was just a little older
than my younger niece
matured early
now everyone noticed
father left alone one morning
never to be seen again
food is scarce at home
mom does her best
but more is needed
across the bar
sits this little angel
who has not even peaked
looks at me while I peek
at a face so beautiful
could have pig tails
but instead looks grown
drinking with a foreigner
smiling as his hand
caresses her back
I'm immediately saddened
as they leave
knowing what's about to happen

Excerpts from Conversations with the Author:

> *"What I don't like to do with creativity is to rush it, it's not really what I do. I like writing, I enjoy it."*

The Son

Dumped

Mom, please don't leave me
here of all places
I'm sure whatever it is
we can work it out
I know we haven't
known each other long
not many people
even know of my existence
including grandma and grandpa
I promise if you take me
I'll be the man my father couldn't
I'm begging you
it's cold and lonely here
I don't think anyone
will find me or even know to look
understand that this is murder
you're killing me slowly
we're both babies
you're not too much older
we can take care of each other
you're not in this alone
one day you'll rely on me
as I do you
on this cold winter day
you're crying, which means
that you do care
yes, just hug me
and forget about this crazy idea
of abandoning your son
great we can go home
wait, mom what are you doing
thought we were past this
no, please pick me back up
come back, please come back
DON'T LEAVE ME

Competition

I remember you walking away
it was a rainy day
or just maybe
it rained in my imagination
an older version of me
just left out the door
never to return
leaving me
with all that a three-year-old mind
could conceptually comprehend
those were the golden years
you taught me so much
in that post-birth time period
I still use those
valuable life lessons to date
couldn't speak that clearly
but you must have understood
what I was saying
during my one-word sentences
and my emotional fits
not quite the man
that you expected
at least I was able to walk
couldn't run without falling
every few steps
had an unusual liking for milk
sort of perverted
even then I enjoyed
planting my head on the breasts of women
there was this one woman
very beautiful lady

I had a crush on her
since day one
I remember her being your lady
she gave me more attention
you have to admit
I was a little cuter
even though we favored each other
I guess you recognized
our attraction for one another
and you just couldn't take
another man in the midst
that being the reason
for your early departure
is totally understandable
jealously is stronger than hate
she was devastated when you left
I quickly moved into your position
wouldn't you know
after thirty years
we are still together

Children Grow

As a child
you learn to survive
in a world that can be cold
exploited bodies used
exchanging carrots for dreams
dangling in front of wondering eyes
wondering why life is so
costly to the soul
as they get used to paying
non-monetary figures
for basic needs to exist
skin closely hugging the bone
face clean but hands dirty
soiled with traces of grown-ups
unrelated and sometimes
related by more than just blood
entering closed gaps
prematurely being matured
to the life of an adult
role models don't catwalk
but sit and scheme
on the defenseless
that they once defended
the virtue of the next
generations of the scorned
heart molded not to feel
as you now recline
in a wheelchair
having one of these
now fully aged children
push you around
eyes widened in astonishment
when your chair
goes right over the edge

Flight like no other

Come take a vacation
like no other
looking through the eyes
of another
standing on the front
lines of memories
experiencing pain
and pleasure alike
falling in and out
of love, heart shattered
abandoned left alone
resentment and rage
joy and happiness
watching those you love
struggle to survive
tears in a mother's eyes
she has no one to lean on
for support or anything else
just you and the others
growing up a man
among women
seeing the world differently
reaping opportunities
from inopportune scenarios
creativity is exercised
make it to the airport
before you miss
the long-awaited flight

Son to Father

You ever thought
why I am
what I am
watching you
while growing
into this state
of adulthood?
looking at the infidelities
witnessing the arguing
seems like you to walk out
and not return for days at a time
how come it's dark
bills late as usual
I think mom's had enough
she's the backbone but now paralyzed
you put her there
now I am here
son to father
unstable as ever
beloved is telling me
I have commitment issues
can't stay long in one place
get bored
so I pick up and leave
that's me
his father's son
no excuses
it's raining outside
and I'm walking
without an umbrella
thanks to yours truly

Self-Cultivate

Self-cultivation
was first discovered
as a pre-teenaged boy
washing away
the memories of yesterday
the thought of a crush
slowly drips down
causing a physical reaction
to the moment
he touches only to soothe
but that in turn
only calls for more touch
hard to calm down
body wet and soapy
he tries to firmly grip
but his hands slide away
the sensation
from the slippage, unbelievable
never felt previously
similar to an annoying itch
that feels good to scratch intensely
fiendishly rubbing
natural instinct is exercised
in unfamiliar new territories
now discovered
heart rapidly beating
momentous is the occurrence
then it finally happens
body involuntarily twitching
close to euphoria
quickly snaps back
into reality
as someone knocks
on the bathroom door

Troubled Youth

It's the ability
for one person
to change another's life
totally unrelated and random
in action, thought and deed
a troubled young man
unhappy with the world
feels owed and unpaid
debts from society
finds comfort with similar minds
framed in a walking cage
false assumptions of freedom
walking along an obscure
long journey to nowhere
whatever he sees
he needs, he grabs
this time was different
met a slight resistance
with a mother of one
offspring watching
tearing at the sight of a stranger
inflicting harm to his only protector
and guardian known
as she falls
the still troubled teen
looks into the eyes of himself
a lot younger and yet to be owed
by the world
up until this shared moment in time

Teenage Hopeful

A teenage hopeful
moved by the same forces
that plague others
walking within his group
girls are women
and he is a man
that decides to take a wife
along a journey
really a girlfriend
but they are acting
twice their age
birthdays come and go
then he penetrates
a seed is now growing within
soon a baby begotten from babies
boy with manly responsibilities
high school why bother
and college a forgotten dream
work becomes harder
reminiscing of his childhood
as he lifts his daily load
heavy things
jeans and boots now dirty
he is finally the man
he was rushing to be

Conversations with a Dead Man

It was my lover
that had the conversation
which I was unable to have
as she sat across
staring at my father
the man who changed my diapers
and saw my first steps
they talked for hours
exchanging stories
of things in common
laughing like old friends
then parted
never to speak again
months later
I learned of the meeting
curious as to what was said
she told an audience
of two as we listened
attentively watching
her every movement
as she looked at
his wife and son
referring to the man
she spoke of
in an unfamiliar name
but only unfamiliar to his son
as he looked at both of them
puzzled and confused only by
the words of his wife
I too see him
since he passed years ago

Boys and Serial

As a boy I would
run around the house
hiding the underwear
in my mother's dressers
burying my sister's dolls
welts on my back
full length legs of redness
trailing down to my ankles
a father that wanted
a masculine son
I just couldn't measure
so I didn't
no longer tried
I saw his face
staring at my makeup-filled face
for the first time
in a life plagued with confusion
tears in the eyes of my mother
rage in the eyes of my father
that later manifested
into something physical
couldn't they see the inner
feelings that I outwardly expressed
I should have gotten help then
now on death row
with psychiatrists trying to figure out
how it happened
I just laughed
and said the word, "ignored"
big bold signs in the making
of an American serial killer

The Convincer

Come on
we been going together
for six months
let's do it
I love you
I promise it won't hurt

I think we should wait
I don't want to get pregnant
my mom will kill me
You've been patient but
I'm scared

scared of what
don't worry
I'm here for you
you won't get pregnant
I'll use a condom

so you have it all figured out

yes, I do
just trust me
no one will be home until later
let's go to my room
don't be scared baby
I'll be gentle

ok, but if it starts to hurt
please stop

ok, I will
let me help you with your jeans

I could get my own jeans
just make sure that the condom
is on correctly

are you ready?

wait, that's not it
right there
wait it hurts

I'll stop but I won't take it out
you'll get use to it
you'll see

it really hurts

ok, baby one second
I am all the way in now

not so hard

ok, I'll go slow
right there
you feel so good

are you done yet

wait, give me a minute
right there, oh, right there
I'm about to
yes, that felt good

ok, take it out now

it's out

where is the condom?

damn, it must of broke

Excerpts from Conversations with the Author:

> *"We have happy times. We have great times. We have fun times. But sometimes things happen. Sometimes ice cream does melt"*

The Lover

Bird

A bird flew
soaring through the blue
of the sunny skies
looking over mountains
on top of trees
quietly landing
to taste the earth in spring
fascinated by the walkers
as they played along
the fields of grass
got too close
and a rock crashed
into the majestic bird
frightened by the action
the bird clumsily flew away
not as high as before
but enough to get away
after months of healing
the bird vowed
never to get close
to a walker again

Boy Meets Girl

Boy meets girl
boy marries girl
and they live happily
ever after and after
but what if boy brings another
into what was held so sacred
are they still in bliss?
or if girl just stops giving boy
what he was so used to getting
boy is now frustrated
girl could even bring another
boy and girl
now have issues
boy loses his job
girl supports boy
but treats boy
similar to a little boy
boy argues with girl
boy and girl
create baby
baby needs milk
money is short
boy starts drinking
girl cries at night
boy hits girl
girl goes to mommy
boy begs her to come back
girl and boy
are not so happy

Déjà vu

You are déjà vu
your look
reminds me
your smell
touch
caressing loses me
your smile
the way your dimples
effortlessly indent
into that so familiar
smooth complexion of skin
strikingly amazing
the resemblance caused
double takes on sight
its been so long
but with you
it seems
like just minutes ago
right before you left
on your way out
now back again
beside me as usual
here to tell the untold silence
as the world waits patiently
for stories
that will never be uttered
these were the tales
that you took
along with your own life

The Evil Doctor

An evil doctor retaining pleasure
From fixing broken hearts
and nursing victims to life
only to puncture their hearts
with a sharp sword once healed
opening wounds that since closed
reveling in their pain and misery
right before the end
he performs another life-saving procedure
to fix the afflicted wound
once again his magic works
his patient is saved
only to suffer the same fate
of a broken heart once again
a vicious cycle indeed
until one day
the patient strikes back
with a sharper sword
right into the chest
of the evil doctor
as the doctor waits to be saved
no one is there to fix his broken heart

The Ring

There once was a ring
which embraced the finger
of a young lady
who showed the ring to everyone
friends were in marvel
envious were some
others in shock
defining true love
in relation to the ring
frowned on their mates
for not presenting them
with a such a ring
one friend, who wore no ring
was happy for her friend
and happy with her mate
the three would often laugh
and sit together
years passed and the young
turned old in age
as the three laughed
yet again as they once did
the question arose
whatever happened to that beautiful ring?
with a sly smirk
the old lady said
I pawned it years ago
the three then laughed
and watched the sunset

Married Strangers

After all of these years
courtship and then
starting a life
mostly for better or worse
all in at this point
you have changed
you're not the person
I once knew and fell into
far from rational
we pulled each other
closer and closer
and now we are here
far from where it first started
feels like the beginning
of the final chapter
wish I would have known
prior to all that transpired
so transparent now
water-glass clear
you are yourself
a stranger in my presence
standing here on this day
such a different person
from that long ago
wedding day

Loners' Vacation

Who wants another one
to be the one
that sheds waterfalls
over smooth peaks
of beautiful scenery
destroying the essence
of what was once pure
scarring the earth
never to heal
what was smooth
became coarse
hardened by the experience
that started sweet
only to turn bitter
at an unforeseen ending
now that it is here
we leave saddened
both for different reasons
vowing never to be the one
on either side of such a mountain
that will scare off future tourists
from what was once a good vacation

Historic Relationship

Think our issue
is what keeps us
coming back for more
forever more the victim
of loving another person
because of who they are
and also due to history
the memories that are
shared and remembered
hated and lamented
so much a part
of who we are
same as us knowing ourselves
before our current state
multiplied by the various
states that embody
all the words that define
our names, likes and dislikes
everything changed over the years
over and over again
but still not gaining a future
just a past that we could remember
and use to get into
the here and today
but we don't stay
until the sun sets
just a day trip
laughing about the past
alone again for breakfast
adding another event
to our historic episode

Dream Guy is Boring

Knight in shining armor
collide with vagabonds
where little princesses
wait to be rescued
damsels in distress
stuck in castles
waiting for their prince of dreams
thoughts of him
make knees weak
now he is here
willing to do whatever
whenever it needs to be done
over and over again
beck and call doorman
service to the privileged
months later now awakened
eyes wide open
without signs
of the night before
situations are now boring
for he is not challenging
pretty easy to control
puppet on a string of pearls
out late night in the rain
you get approached
by a common vagabond
instantly turned on and happy
not to see dream guy

Disease

Heart broken and shattered
from a truth once told
you offered a piece of yourself
enough to contaminate
and nourish simultaneously
concurrently causing opposite
effects to the extreme
I trusted you and dared you
to bare your soul
for one a new beginning
another an old reminder
a conversation that will soon
take place and take time
to explain and examine
the reasons and the feelings
the tears and the remorse
now another to join
a club so sacred
turn around and look
into the eyes of the person
that you just killed

Electronic Love

Do those serendipitous moments
of a once-seen time
still happen in these modern days?
where people meet through
electronic air waves
coursing through a network
moving with light
beaming through the sky
winds blowing messages
birds used to fly
letters of love
one sight
and love is made
two lives intertwined
after one meeting
features of offspring
envisioned within
the minds of the new
union formed from the first
looking good
is what she thought
beautiful
is what he thought
infatuation mentally captured
this is a past time
that we no longer know
maybe forgot fast forward
up late night
can you send a pic
via email?

Friends Lovers Then Friends

We finally found
what the other
was looking for
known for years
as we got to know
the thoughts of the other
intimate friends in between relationships
sometimes even during commitments with others
knowledge of the most scandalous secrets
buried underneath mountains
of a long lasting friendship
could talk about anything
even the attraction shared
and how others viewed it
amazing the simplicity
of candid expression
while looking at the positives
it's hard to find a negative
so this could be it
as ideas crossed
the minds of both
laughter soon after
realizing that neither
would ever fully trust the other

Love on The Run

I remember Love being wanted
on the run, chased by authorities
Love broke the heart of an elderly victim
left motionless in a crime of passion
then took off into the shadows of night
disguised as Hate,
which was felt by mourners
unrecognizable to some
familiar to others
Love walked a thin line
past posted mug shots
all across stationary stores
and other specialty shops
the word is out now
tired and low on resources
the final seconds of freedom
now creeping in
thoughts of a peaceful
surrender is for cowards
utters Infidelity
a new-found friend
the two are strangers
until now
but both are wanted

Man Wants a Woman

You can tell
when a man wants a woman
when he really wants the woman
he looks at her
a certain way
then he does everything
in his power
to get the woman
now he has the woman
but now that he has the woman
it's not the same feeling
it's a different feeling
she is not the same
as before he had her
she is now different
he is now different
in the way he's acting
not the same as before
he is now wanting other women
to keep around at all times
damn, what happened?

Newness

What is it
that you want?
accurate directions
to where needs are met
wants are satisfied
and then changed sporadically?
leaving nothing to desire
bored with everything
the newness
so temporary
once known
and explored?
thoughts of leaving
a situation now old
just turned
just learned
wish to be forgotten
so the good feeling
can again return
that wonderful warm
heart-racing
mind-scrambling
feeling that is now short-lived
most things need and want that
a ceiling out of reach
and no ladder in sight

Time Snatcher

You once called me a time snatcher
all because of the time
that we spent together
you see, over time feelings grew
laughing through happy times
and dealing with sad times
thinking, these are the times
to remember and savor
because times like this
don't come around often
as times changed
so did the feelings
and then the time came
when time apart was needed
hoping to get back together
all in due time
the school of thought was that
time heals all
but after it was over
all that was said was
you wasted my time

Used to You

He doesn't say
what he used to
because he's used to you
in the beginning flowers at work
now a phone call
will do in the afternoon
picking you up
but now the bus
meeting you at home
asking what's for dinner
home-cooked meals turned takeout
transitions of love
are new to old
this is us
building something
or knocking down cities
rebuilding towns
small communities
but we're still
living right here

Warm Body to Hunt

The night turns strangers
into friends for the evening
the quest for a warm body
an additional heartbeat
to add to the rhythmic
sounds of your own
undeniably human in nature
to seek another
even for a short time
unknown communication
through animalistic gestures of reproduction
but not intended to multiply
just feel good
sometimes great or bad
depending on reason of engagement
strangers to companions
back to strangers
recognize the hunt at night
feast on your prey
the morning will bring a new meal

Waterbed

An empty waterbed
with dirty sheets
scented from when last I had company
mementos of a lonely heart
confined to a room
closed in by walls
trapped in a mental prison
of lost love and fond memories
holding onto objects
that contain links
to a past once known
forgotten by others
remembered by the one
who writes in isolation
left talking in the air
echoes are repeated
when empty words are uttered
just a thought of sanity
lonely since it left me
waking up across the side
where the other had fallen
many times on the waterbed
which is now empty and dirty

We Made Love Once

We made love once
had sex, penetration
explored and shared insecurities
securing nothing from the other
excitement resonated when a voice
was just heard in the wind
a faint echo among crowds
wanting only time
savoring the moment
tasting every morsel
and loving the way it went down
sit back and wonder
how those same feelings
turned to irritation
annoyed on impact
avoidance is now a routine
faces are frowned
eyes are rolled
far from ecstasy
puzzling is the paradox
can the original be explored
maybe just a small percent
that can result in
if anything
a friendly conversation

You're a Movie

My mind is plagued with thoughts of you
movie-like in nature
you are the film star
I sat and watched
your entire filmography
playing in my mind
as others look on
attempting to read my face
mind your business
displaying happy and sad thoughts
from the first movie
to your most recent ones
earlier in your career
comedy was your forte
then you got more dramatic roles
which required tears on cue
almost won an academy award
think I was your biggest fan
now sitting alone
in the midst of a mental theater
where popcorn dreams are not allowed
just empty thoughts of happiness
the isolation of loneliness
the pain of an unforgiving heart

Excerpts from Conversations with the Author:

"Words are defined, not people"

The Professional

Glass Ladders

I knew the plan
but deviated
'cause it seemed too easy
go to school and be like us
soon you'll finish up
get a job and move up
ladders made of glass
on the way up
take off your shoes
planks are kinda fragile
if they break
you'll lose your grip
and start from the bottom
saw those who fell
they couldn't climb
once had their youth, strength and vigor
now they're a little feeble
back on the ladder
alongside the youthful
who soon will fall
and have to climb
just as their predecessors
the cycle continues
few avoid this path
and some retire rich

Long work day

Long day of work
one of the hottest summer days
spent hovering over clueless clients
watch as they go through their day
forgetting not remembering
nor thanking you for keeping
your side of the deal
twelve hour days
even working weekends
your colleagues unwilling to help
you through the rain
turning their backs to you
yet you appear everyday
what saves you?
consistent sleep patterns
up early, back to bed early
for you, timing is everything
there for pleasure or pain
as some curse your name
its a shame you're alone
with only one skill to hone
gained respect for your bright attitude
clothed or nude
few can tell the difference
married to your career
spoils with no mate to share
alone but still making it happen
keep shining my friend
for you there will be no relaxing

Never Enough

I've been here before
looking for something
only found at the bottom
unreachable is the pit
but we are falling faster and faster
trying to grab the prize
it will be appreciated
now that it is captured
more is wanted
excitement is no more
only temporary
next to instantaneous
then what ?
question asked
never answered
or truthfully responded
we lie to ourselves
in relaxing settings
planning everything
and doing exactly
what was planned
finally made it
more plans are now needed
I've been here before
that empty feeling
looking for something
only found at the bottom
unreachable is the pit

Broker of Pleasure

I'm from the school of thought
that people need people
moreover a man needs a women
I mean, wars were fought for such things
you see every need
needs three things
supply, demand and someone
to introduce the two
that's my role
a broker of pleasure
one who seizes
the opportunity
to link two entities
in a safe environment
for a modest commission
like any other profession
it requires finesse and skill
notice the word profession
other people have such
derogatory terms for a trade
that's been going on since the beginning of time
I'm a mere middleman
in a very complicated exchange

Bartender

They are story takers
silently providing an ear
to those that seek
to be listened to
some tales are sad
some are happy
regardless of the ending
they hear everything
creating an atmosphere
where some are comfortable
others off balance
dazed off of fluids
used by the gods
to battle with demons
that now possess
the humblest of men
whose talk seduces
the curiosity
igniting wondering questions
that can't be asked
they must volunteer
a live documentary
giving more stories
for the story taker
to take as their own

Child at Work

You realize your daily interactions
are not that important
not in the grand scheme
of how things turn
as the world tosses
and turns spinning in circles
around the feeble-minded individuals
looking in awe amazed
at what they see
you feel like a newborn
fresh to the arena at large
watched by spectators
and gladiators alike
all observing each movement
attentive to the folds
and creases of your skin
yet to hear you speak
is a true surprise and annoyance
you are shunned like a child
in an adult conversation
laughing at the situation
yet made to feel small
grown ups in car seats
but you are being compensated
does feel like enough?

Defining Life

For many things
And many people
definitions are inapplicable
doing one thing
is way too simple
no matter how complex the action
it's eventually understood
waking up to the same perfunctory action
some are passionate
and couldn't picture themselves
in another pose
but why not push beyond the boundaries
the world is big enough and round in shape
unlike the flat surface
it was once thought to be
so should life be flat and boxed-shaped
with the lid closed?
filled with foam?
suspending the experts of the world perfectly in the
middle?

Killing Time

How do you kill time?
something so everlasting yet elusive and swift
hard to catch sometimes
and even harder to find
we study it
we beat it
yet it still ticks
analogous to heart beats
with an intimidating presence
only to those that use it advantageously
for they are scared to lose and always want more
for they have no desire to harm such an ally
looking to the past with a smile and good memories
waiting for the future with anticipation
thinking about all there is to do
they are content with the relationship
while others feel cheated
not happy with the present
unable to change the past
feel that time should go back
mad because it can't
so they just sit
thinking of ways to kill time

Biz Night Out

I listen to the conversation
it is fake
business in a social scene
how ironic is that?
just talking about nothing
but we are all here
watching, drinking and listening
to what is going on
really nothing important
as steam rises
stress is temporarily
put on hold
until the morning
this is the night out

Observing Streets after Work

Just left one night
not in a rush
no car, train or bus
to my destination
just a long walk
down a traveled path
observing the life
which I'm often flying past
mind free, wind blowing
saw a man so impressed with a free dollar
that it brought a smile to his face
with many thank you-s
saw a couple that needed
money for kung fu lessons
to avenge their parents' death
at the hands of a ninja
drug-induced of course
but ever so entertaining
as I walked thinking of what I missed
trapped within an office cubicle
only in the streets of Manhattan

Office Meeting

Meetings after meetings
executive chairs and projectors
water cooler conversation
answers to questions just to respond
questions asked just because
the lingo must keep going
the jokes must persist
sort of like high school again
same tendencies
ten year reunion approaching
same meeting hours later
some just look
some just talk
some just sleep
quickly awakening
with a gesture, laugh or nudge
change of topic, a clap
is the conclusion near?
is this life?

People Defined

What happens
when a single point
defines your existence
or explains to everyone
exactly what your are about
then magically one day
that part of your life
ceases to exist
are you now undefined?
a word without meaning
is not a word by definition
this is true
do you no longer exist?
has the point escaped
from a life
that is now shallow
unfulfilled and unexplained?
you are now
just here to assist in watching others
looking them up and reading
their definitions out loud

A Quick Stint

It was suppose to be a quick stint
I was promised the riches of a king
the perks of a corporate executive
what an opportunity
all he asked for was my soul
and the dreams that were once occupants
of this happy haven
favorite memories and thoughts of the future
visited by inspiration
and the faith of my forefathers
courage of fallen warriors
yet the tenderness of a mother
with a newborn son
a gentrifying neighborhood
minds of low and high income
earners alike in the same park
slowly losing the distinction
a now quick stint
can be measured in years
left with a handsome ransom
and an unoccupied soul

Race

In the midst of the race
stood a motionless observer
watching patiently
as others ran breathless
bumping into each other
some even hurdling
over the fallen bodies
amused by the man
effortlessly standing
the runners laughed
and ridiculed him
during each circle around
tripping over the fellow racers
old and young alike
such a brutal race
where participation was
surprisingly voluntary
everyone racing for the varied
rewards that life had to offer
"BE CAREFUL" shouts a judge
as a runner trips over another
still standing is the man watching
asking only for water
so he too can eventually
rejoin the race

Another Kind of Race

You see yourself
among your peers
that's how the race is measured
those similar in strength
age, intellect, and chances
could be anything
and now they're winning
and you're not
not because of speed
you just stopped running
didn't even feel like walking
just stood there watching
as they kept going
you're now squinting your eyes
because they're too far ahead
to see clearly
frustrated by your current situation
you decide to join a new race
one just starting
not there to compete
just to hold others up
delaying them from running
offering only distractions
in the form addictive substances
you teach the boys
how to play the sidelines
and still keep up
you teach the girls
how to push strollers
another form of exercise
you now have company
unfortunately bored
with the current conversation
you fade into the stands and marvel
at what you just created

Superior

Know your place
in the hierarchal system
where fate meets life
now just following
someone deemed superior
in the current state
you find yourself looking
upward towards this person
or better yet him
looking downward
towards you
amazing that one would think
they are above another
control met by monetary advances in career
maybe a title or two
not fully understanding
that life is so much bigger
than these four walls
on judgment day
will you still reign superior to all
that you currently oversee
or pay money for services rendered
on a daily basis?

Pile of Life

So this is what you put
on the cold ground
then took a few steps
backwards alone in silence
looking at all that came hard
a few feet away is everything
that defined your purpose up until now
staring at it in amazement
a tear trickles down
salty is the taste
mind over yonder
thinking was it really
worth all that was done?
looking at all the luxuries
amidst the pain
sleepless nights
apologies and good byes
alongside broken hearts
mixed in with one to two regrets
laughing hysterically
wishing to trade in all the misery caused
for the prizes resting adjacent to the losses
naked now baring only the truth within words

Excerpts from Conversations with the Author:

> *"The one thing that I fear in life, two things: I fear God and I fear prison"*

The Prisoner

Beast of a Man

The beast of a man
and now you're tanned
you all look alike
in this concrete jungle
by other species
you're deemed as the weakest
our prey we kill
Their pulse stopped beating
blood fresh as day
you eat at tables
your victims well done
using kitchen utensils
our teeth still red from the bite
of some new found flesh
yeah, you bite the flesh
but wash your mouths
to cover up the stench
We roll in packs
you stand aside
and watch one another
if trouble comes
you run and tell
someone that is stronger
in a lawless land
left alone
you'll probably be ripped apart
funny how
you convinced yourselves
that this is called civilized

Tears Stop Falling

Tears stopped falling
memories became pictures
frozen in time
a shell of me
past to present
age and wisdom
regret everything and nothing
all at the same time
a lifetime has past
but my life continues
the older ones remember
the younger ones don't know me
I am not there anymore
I am here now
for I survived
and wish no man
such a fate
of an adulthood tucked away
where society
can't reach you
family can't see you
it's now my time
and their time too

Behind in Debt

Trapped without bars
or regulated schedules
confinement and violence
trapped instead with interests
mortgages car payments loans
high habits expensive taste
with good restaurants
have to stay the course
deviation could cause bankruptcy
escape from reality for just a second
letters are stacked up beyond belief
mixed with late charges
penalties for any delay
keep running the circle
of a paid existence
getting up to do
what does not come naturally
you are here
for what greater purpose?
a prisoner of debt
congratulations
you did not make it

Dry Land

I'm standing at the edge
of shelter and rain
watching others get wet
not necessarily
blocking the entrance
but not opening the door
just standing as they scramble
maneuvering between droplets
some are lucky
and manage to stay dry
the majority are not
they get drenched
my friends laugh
as they get close
and turn them away
mocking them as they turn
their backs to dry land
slowly walking towards
unbreathable locations
tired from the confusion
some just quit
and stand motionless
waiting for the water
to hit their dry skin
as tears run down
the cheeks of men, women
children no longer young
hearts are cold
eyes have seen plenty
can't tell what hurts more
getting all wet up
or being turned away
by their own people

Free Enough

Ever felt free
you know free enough
to make a decision
that the outcome
could be anything
and land you anywhere
yes I remember that day
when all seemed lost
so it was whatever
then came the option
presented over a drink
and I said whatever
seemed like a good idea
at the time I was younger
full of unlimited energy
why was she so scared
we were suppose to be
in and out in less
than five minutes
the security guard
came out of nowhere
don't go for your firearm
I must have of got to mine first
impulse is involuntary
most of the time at least
sad the judge didn't agree
twenty five years later
I'm now talking to you
can't be more than twenty five
young in the face
so what are you in for?

Prison Trilogy
—part 1

Street survivalist
born walking over get-right vials
to far out destinations
looking up to jewels
and shiny wheels
on luxury mobiles
living in a box
publicly assisted
hard to resist
temptation everywhere
frail in size but outspoken
heavy with heat
loud noises go bang bang
the crowd quickly ducks
he's laughing at life
sun radiating over teeth
covered with gold
not for the taking
quick-tempered
a strategic facade
used to hide fear
then came graduation
no diploma on this day
instead snow
enough to fill a pack
noticed by the overseers
he is captured
first time offender
gone until adulthood

—part 2

Institution of higher learning
first day at school
the other kids are watching
while the teachers are monitoring hallways
once cleared
everyone sits in their new class
a newly transferred student
feels out of place
once outspoken and loud
he is now quiet and humble
observant of his new surroundings
a few kids pick on him
just to get a reaction
they are then brushed away
by an older child
that takes a liking
to the new student
the two laugh
and become friends
one-sided gifts
consisting of pens, notepads
and even cancer sticks
are exchanged
hesitant
but then accepting of these tokens
with nothing to offer in return
the naive newcomer
expresses his gratitude
pretty cool how the other children
some more fierce
don't bother the newcomer
his new friend
clearly marks his ground

as the sun rises
on an arbitrary Sunday
the once-happy older friend seems perturbed
and starts demanding all of his gifts back
confused, the newcomer apologizes
and promises
to repay the gratitude in time
but the time has already come
off guard with nothing to offer
he is struck swiftly across the head
followed by hard shots to the abdomen
rendered close to unconscious
he feels his clothes being undone
feebly tries to resist
but he his struck
on the back of the head
face bounced from the floor
nose bleeding on impact
unbelievable what he is feeling
cries for help are ignored
as he is entered
pleasured is his new friend
other guests begin to arrive
he has now been marked
by the school predators

— part 3

As the years pass
another graduation day
has arrived
school is now over
the new child
is now a grown man
let back into the world
walking back over
the get right vials
into the publicly assisted box-like buildings
he is left to his own devices
meets up with old friends
discusses ways to get
what he's been missing
feeling different about life
has emotional issues
from past experiences
relationships with the opposite sex
kind of different
doing things that won't cause procreation
looking at younger men differently
a strange attraction
overcomes him secretly
not admitting
trapped in his own mind
full circle
with an empty existence
health checks seem abnormal
could have been infected?
with nothing to lose
feels bullish for risky investing
gambles on a caper
that crapped out

in front of a judge yet again
in the same life
no sorry excuses
or tears passing down
just waiting
for his new job
he made good
a student teacher assignment
at his old Alma mater

Ready For Society

Permission to breathe, please
while we're are at it
need to defecate
along with a little urination
you have me under complete
total, bottle full, control
I am yours and also his
or whoever I am passed to
need license plates
or tending to the field
let me assist
as years and days
pass along a timeline
so does my youth and vigor
I'm a broken human being
that volunteers myself to pass time
something to do among others
like self defense
a basic human instinct
survival among beasts
now older and wiser
heartless and cold
I am now ready for society
from my whole eyes leaked pity
upon soul survivors
of an incarcerated city

POW

Now that sides don't matter
it is over
all that was going on outside
reasons and motives are forgotten
only reality left
the circumstance of a decision
that wasn't yours originally
became yours eventually
now you are trapped
among similar folks
that once stood side to side
and fought until there was nothing left
it is now that you are remembered
by those that feel the pain of a world gone
and those that hold the key to your physical freedom
they can't forget while they stand there
watching over and torturing the flesh
of the battle that claimed
lives on both ends
where is the cavalry?
home enjoying their families
for them it is all over
a distant memory
that changed the definition
of a word called life
some for the better
some for the worse
others permanently fell
into other realms of existence
wishing to join them soon
but it is not your time
still more to go
an unfortunate commonplace
when kids fight
both never stop
at the same time

Balancing Act

Saw a man
walk a straight line
on a narrow path
trying to keep balanced
and still progress
it became an almost impossible task
just maintaining
easy to some but difficult to this fellow
among various men watching attentively
looking for a slight deviation off course
as difficult as it was
the well-balanced man
completed his journey
and lived happily ever
only after he was released
from prison for being under the influence
while using his vehicle as a device for destruction
and ending a short-lived life
he was left with years to reflect
on a single moment in time
when the world was slightly off balance

Hustler's Gift

Dreams get kissed
a hustlers heart
is his gift
freedom is a price
that costs less
than death
but more than
the life of a snitch
which is worthless
still need the payment in full
plus the vig
can't let nothing slide
once you play
no one wants to go inside
sun up 'til sun down
proceeds in pounds
and other weight denominations
pulled in varying directions
given a choice early
and now you ride
can't get out of the car
while still in mid-drive
wind up hurt or worst
a sacrificed soul
to these streets
where characters meet
bopping their heads
to a cop's beat
silver bracelets glisten
below a flooded arm piece
meeting the sleeve's end

of a hooded fleece
stomach to the pavement
pissed on by crack fiends
that's entry level
for fed time
they come to your residence
knock on your door
with a special invite
given to you upon entrance
you're big time now homie
the fortunes of a community
are now handed over
to your high-priced attorney

The Ending

Five Seconds of Fame

The eve of stardom
right before being known
is cool
plastic surgery without the operation
you appear different to those who know you
your ink engraved mark instantly becomes priceless
a simple photograph is timeless
a vibrating phone transforms into a sensual toy
pulsating against your hip through daily interactions
assumptions become truth
casual acquaintances are synonymous
with intimate bedfellows
in a darkly lit room you shine above all
with good and bad intentions alike
now a target
bull's eye and fame-maker
for someone a little younger
eager for droplets of your rainmaker
so-called fans now torn
another ghetto superstar to mourn

End Notes

Why does ice cream melt?

Information on the melt down process of ice cream was researched from the following site:

http://www.foodsci.uoguelph.ca/dairyedu/icstructure.
html

The Author

Who am I? I'm a person who eats when I'm hungry and drinks when I'm thirsty. I'm the person at the end of the bar who raises his glass to a familiar face. I care about the feelings of the people around me. I love hard and don't forget faces. I get overly excited about new ideas. I could spend hours talking to a stranger, if their story is interesting. I believe in hard work and sacrifice. I think that people spend way too much time defining themselves as oppose to just living. My word is more important than any amount of money. Fear motivates me to reach beyond myself. My heart is pure, but my tongue is corrupted. I am you, him, and her all at the same time.

Let's Keep Touch

Company Website: http://www.IceCreamMelts.com

The full interview, "Conversations With the Author", and other Ice Cream Melts footage is available on www.IceCreamMelts.com.

Please send all inquiries to info@IceCreamMelts.com.